SPOTLIGHT ON SPACE SCIENCE

JOURNEY TO MARS

LORIN GRUBER

New York

Published in 2015 by The Rosen Publishing Group, Inc.
29 East 21st Street, New York, NY 10010

First Edition

Editor: Susan Meyer
Book Design: Kris Everson

Photo Credits: Cover (main), pp. 13, 27 NASA/JPL-Caltech/MSSS; cover (planet Mars), p. 29 NASA/JPL; p. 5 NASA/JPL-Caltech/USGS; p. 7 SCIEPRO/Getty Images; p. 9 NASA/JPL/Texas A&M/Cornell; p. 11 NASA, Jet Propulsion Laboratory; p. 12 NASA/JPL-Caltech/Univ. of Arizona; pp. 15, 17, 19, 21, 25 NASA; p. 23 ASA/JPL/Corby Waste.

Library of Congress Cataloging-in-Publication Data

Gruber, Lorin.
Journey to Mars / by Lorin Gruber.
p. cm. — (Spotlight on space science)
Includes index.
ISBN 978-1-4994-0371-8 (pbk)
ISBN 978-1-4994-0400-5 (6-pack)
ISBN 978-1-4994-0418-0 (library binding)
1. Mars (Planet) — Juvenile literature. 2. Mars (Planet) — Exploration — Juvenile literature. I. Title.
QB641.G78 2015
523.43—d23

Manufactured in the United States of America

CPSIA Compliance Information: Batch #CW15PK: For Further Information contact Rosen Publishing, New York, New York at 1-800-237-9932

CONTENTS

CHAPTER 1

When the ancient Romans looked to the night sky, they saw a light that glowed red. They named this blood-colored light Mars, after their god of war.

The Romans only knew what they could see with their eyes. Today, however, telescopes on Earth, spacecraft **orbiting** Mars and even **rovers** that have landed on Mars have uncovered many of the secrets of the **planet**. Today, we know Mars looks red because the soil on its surface is coated in iron oxide, or rust. We also know that our neighbor in the solar system is much smaller than Earth. It has a diameter of just 4,212 miles (6,779 km), compared to Earth's diameter of 7,918 miles (12,743 km).

Scientists have discovered that the fourth planet from the Sun is home to deserts, giant volcanoes, and vast areas covered with ice. We know more than our sky-gazing ancestors could ever have imagined. However, Mars, or the "Red Planet" as it is sometimes called, still has many intriguing mysteries to be solved!

Today, we have detailed photographs of the crater-covered surface of Mars.

HOW THE SOLAR SYSTEM WAS FORMED

CHAPTER 2

Mars, Earth, and the other planets in the solar system were created when our Sun formed about 4.5 billion years ago.

Before our solar system formed, there was a huge cloud of gas and dust in space. Over time, the cloud collapsed on itself, forming a massive spinning sphere, or ball. Around the sphere, a disk formed from the remaining gas and dust. The sphere pulled in more gas and dust, adding to its size, weight, and **gravity**. Pressure built up in the core, or center, of the sphere, causing the core to get hotter and hotter. Finally, the temperature inside the sphere became so hot that it ignited. A new **star**, our Sun, was born!

Inside the disk of rotating gas and dust around the Sun, other masses formed. These masses became the solar system's eight planets. Mercury is the closest planet to the Sun. Next comes Venus, then Earth, Mars, Jupiter, Saturn, Uranus, and finally Neptune.

The planets are shown here in correct order, but not drawn to scale. Mars is the fourth planet orbiting the Sun.

THE ORBIT AND ROTATION OF MARS

CHAPTER 3

Like all the planets in the solar system, Mars is orbiting the Sun.

The length of time that a planet takes to orbit the Sun is known as a year. For example, a year on Earth lasts for 365 days. Mars is much further from the Sun than Earth, so it takes 687 days to travel around the Sun once. This means a year on Mars is nearly twice as long as a year on Earth.

Like Earth, Mars is slightly tilted on its **axis**. This causes Mars to have seasons. As Mars travels in its orbit, the northern hemisphere, or top half, of the planet begins tilting toward the Sun. This causes temperatures in the northern hemisphere to rise, so it is summer. As Mars moves through its orbit, the southern hemisphere, or bottom half, begins tilting toward the Sun. For this part of the year, the northern hemisphere experiences winter.

A day on Mars is approximately the same as a day on Earth. This photo shows the Sun setting on Mars.

MARS'S MOONS

CHAPTER 4

Mars is not alone as it travels through space. It has two small traveling companions. These are its moons, Phobos and Deimos, which are orbiting the planet.

Phobos and Deimos look like rocky, lumpy potatoes. No one knows for sure how the moons came to be in orbit around Mars. It is likely they are asteroids that came too close to Mars and were captured by its gravity.

Phobos orbits Mars just 3,700 miles (5,955 km) above the planet's surface. It is so close to Mars that it can orbit the planet three times in every 24-hour period. Deimos is further away and takes about 30 hours to make one orbit.

The spacecraft *Mars Express*, which is orbiting Mars and studying the planet, has found evidence that suggests Phobos may not be a single solid rock. It could actually be a collection of smaller rocks and rubble tightly held together by gravity to form a single body.

Gaspra

Deimos

Phobos

These photos, taken by the Viking Orbiter, *show Phobos (lower right) and Deimos (lower left). They are compared here to a large asteroid called Gaspra.*

Just like Earth, Mars is surrounded by an atmosphere made of gases. Mars's atmosphere is about 100 times thinner than Earth's, though.

This image shows a dust devil (viewed from above) traveling across the surface of Mars. The whirlwind of dust was about 0.5 miles (0.8 km) high!

Mars's atmosphere is mostly made of carbon dioxide, with just a small amount of nitrogen and other gases. Unlike Earth's atmosphere, it contains only a trace of oxygen. If humans were ever to visit Mars, they would not be able to stand on the planet's surface and breathe unless they were wearing breathing equipment attached to tanks of oxygen.

The movement of gases in Mars's atmosphere causes winds to blow over the planet's surface, just as movements of air cause wind on Earth. The winds on Mars whip up the dust that covers the planet's surface. These winds often create massive dust storms that can cover the whole planet for weeks.

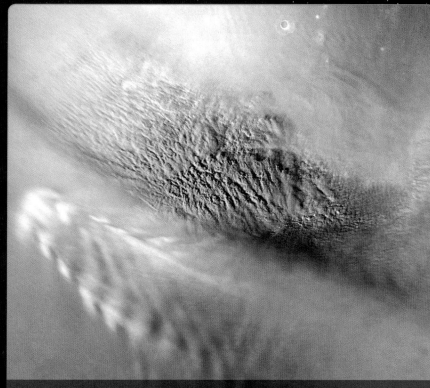

The Mars Reconnaissance Orbiter captured this photo of a dust storm on Mars in 2007.

BENEATH THE SURFACE

The dusty, rocky surface of Mars is a fascinating world of huge impact craters, canyons, and volcanoes.

Beneath the surface, Mars is very similar to Earth. At its center is a solid core of metal made mostly of iron. The core is surrounded by a layer called the mantle. This layer is made up of molten rock and metal. The outer crust of the planet is formed from a thick layer of rock.

The surface of Mars is scarred by many impact craters. These are created when asteroids and **meteoroids** smash into the planet's surface.

Mars is also home to the largest canyon in the solar system, Valles Marineris. The canyon is over eight times the length of the Grand Canyon and in places is over three times as deep! The massive canyon runs along Mars's equator. It probably formed when the planet's outer crust moved and cracked billions of years ago when Mars was still a young planet.

Mars's rough surface, as seen in this image, has been created by space objects striking the planet.

OLYMPUS MONS

CHAPTER 7

Mars is not only home to the solar system's largest canyon—it also boasts the largest mountain on any planet in the solar system.

Olympus Mons is a massive volcano that is 16 miles (26 km) high from its base to its highest point. That's three times the height of Mount Everest, the tallest mountain on Earth!

Olympus Mons is no longer active, or erupting. In its past, however, eruption after eruption poured **lava** from its crater, which then hardened and over time formed the mountain's sloping sides. The volcano is so massive that at its base, the slopes have collapsed under their own weight to form steep cliffs that are nearly 2 miles (3 km) high.

It's hard to imagine the vast size of this monster volcano. If Olympus Mons were set down on Earth, though, it would cover an area the size of Arizona!

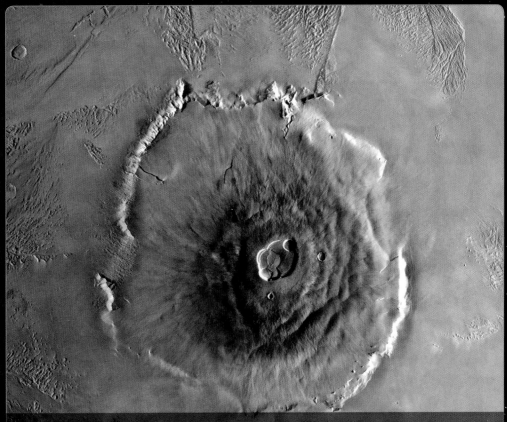

*At the top of Olympus Mons is a **caldera**, seen here, that is 50 miles (80 km) wide!*

LIFE ON MARS?

CHAPTER 8

Since ancient times, people have been watching Mars in the night sky. Over the centuries, some people began to wonder if our neighboring planet might be home to an alien civilization.

In the late 1800s, an Italian astronomer named Giovanni Schiaparelli studied Mars through a telescope. Schiaparelli said he could see strange lines on the planet that he called *canali*, which is the Italian word for "channels." Some people translated *canali* to mean "canals," which are artificial rivers constructed by people. The lines seemed to join at dark, greenish areas on the planet's surface. An American astronomer, Percival Lowell, wrote that the lines could be canals built by Martians to carry water from wet areas to dry places where plants were being grown. His works made this idea very popular.

When spacecraft visited Mars in the 1960s, however, they sent back images of a dry landscape. The canals were just a trick of the light when people looked through telescopes. There were no canals, no plants, and no aliens!

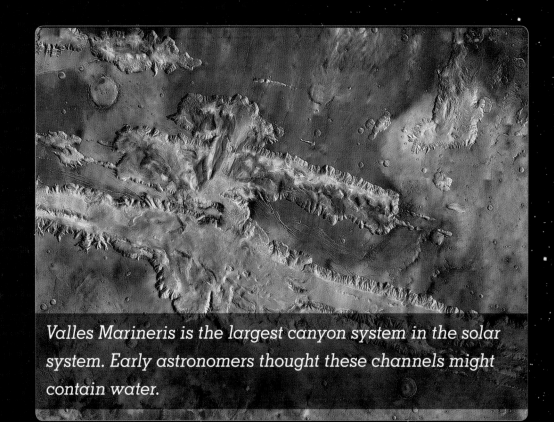

Valles Marineris is the largest canyon system in the solar system. Early astronomers thought these channels might contain water.

FROZEN WATER

When spacecraft began to visit Mars in the 1960s, they didn't find canals, rivers, oceans, or liquid water. There is, however, lots of ice and evidence that there was once liquid water on Mars.

Just like Earth, Mars has large areas of ice, called ice caps, at its north and south poles. The top layer of the ice caps is made up of dry ice, which is frozen carbon dioxide gas. Below the dry ice, however, there is frozen water. There is also lots of frozen water underground, just as there is frozen water in the ground in **Arctic** regions on Earth.

Billions of years ago, however, it was a different story. Valleys carved across the land and marks in rocks show that liquid water once flowed over the planet's surface. Today, Mars is too cold for liquid water to exist. So what caused Mars's climate to change? When did the water

isappear? And was Mars once a water-covered, varm planet like Earth?

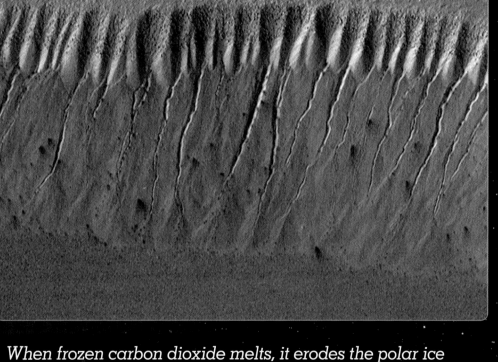

When frozen carbon dioxide melts, it erodes the polar ice caps on Mars, creating the spiderlike formations seen here.

MISSIONS TO MARS

CHAPTER 10

Many spacecraft have been sent to Mars to study the planet. Some have orbited Mars, studying it from space, while others have landed on its surface.

When the orbits of Earth and Mars bring the two planets close together, it can take as little as six months for a spacecraft to reach Mars.

In 1976, the *Viking 1* and *Viking 2* landers were the first spacecraft to land on Mars. The landers photographed the planet's surface and studied its atmosphere and soil.

At the end of 2014, there were five spacecraft orbiting Mars. NASA's 2001 *Mars Odyssey* has been studying Mars since 2001. One of its tasks is to transmit messages from rovers on the surface of Mars back to Earth.

The European Space Agency's *Mars Express* spacecraft has been in orbit since 2003. Part of its mission is to study the history of liquid water on the planet. NASA's *Mars Reconnaissance Orbiter* is looking for evidence of ancient Martian seas and studying changes in Mars's climate.

NASA's *Mars Atmosphere and Volatile EvolutioN Mission* (*MAVEN*) began orbiting Mars and studying its atmosphere in September 2014. The Indian Space Research Organization's *Mars Orbiter Mission* also reached Mars in September 2014.

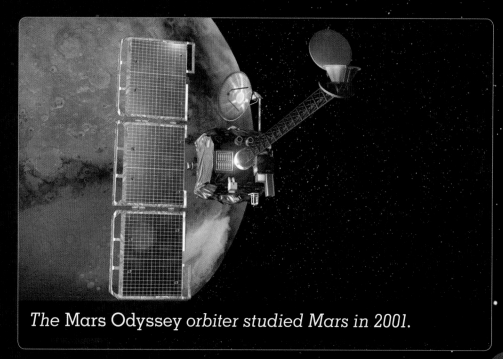

The Mars Odyssey orbiter studied Mars in 2001.

SPIRIT AND OPPORTUNITY

CHAPTER 11

In January 2004, NASA's twin rovers *Spirit* and *Opportunity* landed on Mars on opposite sides of the planet. The mission of the two robotic geologists was to study Mars's rocks and soil for clues about its watery past.

A human geologist walks from place to place examining rocks with handheld tools. In comparison, the robotic rovers were controlled by human operators on Earth and could drive up to 130 feet (40 m) in a day. Each rover was fitted with a robotic arm and many different scientific instruments for studying rocks and carrying out experiments.

During their mission, the rovers have discovered plenty of evidence in Mars's rocks and soil to show that Mars was once a planet with liquid water.

Spirit worked for over six years until it became

stuck in sand and NASA had to terminate its mission. At the end of 2014, *Opportunity* was still exploring the surface of Mars. The robot geologist, which was originally designed to work for just three months, was still going strong!

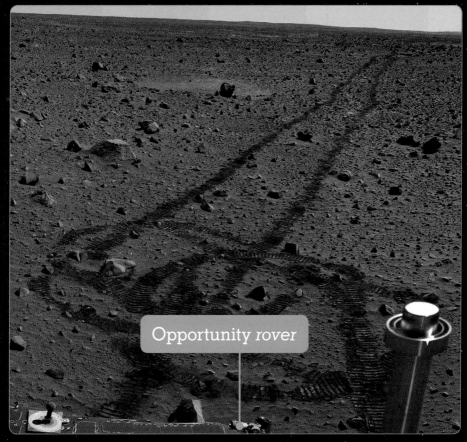

Opportunity rover

This photo was taken by Opportunity *in 2006. The little rover continues to explore Mars almost a decade later.*

CURIOSITY CONTINUES

CHAPTER 12

In August 2012, a robot rover named *Curiosity* landed on the surface of Mars. *Curiosity* is part of NASA's Mars Science Laboratory Mission.

Curiosity is about the size of an SUV. It is a huge vehicle compared to tiny *Sojourner,* the first robot to travel on the surface of Mars, which was about the size of a microwave oven!

Safely encased inside a spacecraft, *Curiosity* blasted out of Earth's atmosphere aboard an Atlas V rocket in November 2011. The spacecraft traveled the millions of miles (km) to Mars and entered the planet's atmosphere. The spacecraft then descended on a parachute. In the final seconds, the descent stage and *Curiosity* emerged from the spacecraft. The descent stage then acted like a crane and lowered *Curiosity* to the ground on tethers.

Curiosity *took this* self-portrait in May 2013.

MYSTERIES OF MARS

CHAPTER 13

Water is essential for living things to survive. If Mars was once a warmer planet and had liquid water, perhaps it was home to living things!

The *Curiosity* rover will analyze soil and rocks on Mars. It will look for chemical clues that Mars could once have been a suitable place for life to exist. If there was life on Mars, it would not have been intelligent alien beings, but microscopic life-forms called **microbes**.

In 1984, scientists found a small **meteorite** that had crashed into Earth from Mars. Inside the rock, they found microscopic tubelike shapes. Some scientists believed the shapes could be the **fossils** of microbes that lived on Mars billions of years ago. Other scientists did not agree with this idea.

The first living things on Earth were microscopic microbes. Was Mars once home to microbes, too?

Millions of miles (km) from Earth, *Curiosity* is searching for clues to help solve the mystery. Will it find signs of microscopic life? Will it find something amazing that we've not yet imagined? Only time and science will tell!

rover tracks

Curiosity and its tracks can be faintly seen on the dusty surface of Mars.

GLOSSARY

Arctic: Referring to the very cold areas around the North Pole.

axis: An imaginary straight line around which a planet turns.

caldera: A large crater that's formed when a large eruption happens, causing a volcano's opening to collapse.

fossil: Hardened remains of plants or animals that lived long ago.

gravity: The force that pulls an object toward the center of another object that has mass.

lava: Melted rock that comes out of a volcano.

meteorite: A piece of matter from space that passes through a planet's atmosphere and strikes the ground.

meteoroid: A small piece of an asteroid that has broken off the main mass.

microbe: A microscopic life-form.

orbit: To move around an object along a curved path; also, the curved path of an object.

planet: A space object that orbits a star.

rover: A remote-controlled vehicle that explores the surface of other planets.

star: A space object made of gases that produces its own light.

FOR MORE INFORMATION

BOOKS

Aguilar, David A. *Space Encyclopedia: A Tour of Our Solar System and Beyond.* Washington, D.C.: National Geographic, 2013.

Carney, Elizabeth. *Mars.* Washington, D.C.: National Geographic, 2014.

Rusch, Elizabeth. *The Mighty Mars Rovers: The Incredible Adventures of Spirit and Opportunity.* New York, NY: Houghton Mifflin Books for Children, 2012.

WEBSITES

INDEX